AF413143

BOLD &
CHOSEN

BOLD &
CHOSEN

LILLIE DIAZ

atmosphere press

© 2024 Lillie Diaz

Published by Atmosphere Press

Cover design by Felipe Betim

No part of this book may be reproduced without permission from the author except in brief quotations and in reviews.

Atmospherepress.com

I want to dedicate this book to my Father. You deserve all the glory and praise for what you have done in my life. I am forever yours, and let your will be done, not mine. Thank you for loving me when I couldn't love myself.

Table of Contents

POETRY

Love Letter to My Father

Have you ever written a love letter to someone? And didn't know
what to say?
I'm a little nervous, but the voice of the holy one will lead my
words to the way.
Growing up, I went through things a child shouldn't go through;
My mom wasn't listening when I needed someone to talk to.
Surrounded by confusion and noise, I couldn't understand,
That all that was happening was by the hand of a distorted, angry man.
I would go to church and wonder why this was happening to me;
Everyone else seemed so happy. How could that be?
Growing up, I looked for happiness in things that were temporary fun,
Men, alcohol, drugs, cigarettes, pills, but I was still unhappy when
it was all said and done,
Making decisions I am not proud of making,
Doing things for the thrill of not truly knowing what I was deeply
seeking,
I was looking for a love so deep you only hear about it in fairy tales.
Little did I know there was a king whose heart held me with a
love that never fails,
Me, I wondered, *you died for me? A sinner who struggles and falls short
every day*
Behold, I have made you new in this life, he said, I will lead your way.
I can't believe it—this is the love I have been searching for,
The love I sought and desired to fight for me was already waiting
at the door.
I couldn't believe my king was here with me all this time I felt so
alone,
He was always right behind me, reigning on his throne.

I will never forget the moment Jesus made his presence known to me;
I was in church and finally raised my arms to the one who set me free.
He died on the cross, took away my past sin and shame,
That moment the old me died and I was given a new name;
Bride to be, bride to come, make way, make way for the holy one,
Whose blood was shed for you and me, he's coming back to set the
    captives free, the war is done,
The enemy has no power, no authority over children of the highest.
Don't worry, weary one, the lake of fire is waiting for him in this
    coming time,
I feel something manifesting inside me I won't deny anymore,
The mighty name of Jesus; hear his power in my voice roar.
Hallelujah to the king of kings,
I am preparing for your coming and what your peace will bring.
I will surrender my worries, fears in due time,
Never mind you didn't give me a spirit of fear but a spirit of love,
    power, and a sound mind.
I claim an anointing over my words to touch others by the hands
    of our creator,
He is my healer, physician, chain breaker—never again will I need
    a mediator.
I will not be silent or ashamed to praise or spread your glorious name,
The joy and peace I claim in your mighty name will not be contained.
Jesus's last words were to the world *It is finished,*
Never in this world or the heavens will his words be diminished.
We have to fight back with the word of God that is our weapon
    and daily bread,
To fight the good fight and always know what Jesus said.
He loves us so much to follow his father's will and lose his life,
Will you take the next step for everlasting life?

The Rise of Christ

I can't believe my ears, I can't believe what I see,
The one who created the wind and sea is right beside me.
He rose from the grave, defeated death and made himself known,
The good news is this horrible place isn't our home.
Christ gave us hope for victory over the grave,
Not even the Romans had the stone contained.
The rise of Christ was the moment his spirit came to live here on Earth,
It was a momentary death preparing for his rebirth.
Son of the living God who bore the cross has prepared the way for you,
There is no sea, no grave, no mountain that he cannot move.
Our Father who art in heaven, hallowed be thy name,
The moment he gave up his son, things would never be the same.
2,000 years ago Christ suffered for our sins and deceitful behavior,
Thank the lord our God he has sent us a savior.
The king who set the captives free is alive and well,
When two or more are gathered he is in the midst, can't you tell?
The miracle worker who heals, saves, frees, and delivers,
Can make anyone question their belief and make them reconsider.
One touch on the heart can make a drastic change in one's life,
The holy spirit living inside you can turn you away from wrath,
    anger, and strife.
I believe his word and know he rose from that tomb,
Never will I doubt the one who created me in my mother's womb.
Praise Ye, says the people of Jerusalem,
Make way for the one who came back home again.
His word remains thousands of years later by the words of his
    followers and father,
One day he will descend from the clouds and we will all be together.

Dear Father

I can't believe this is happening, what makes me count to the one above?

Though dirty and stained, filthy wretch, he sustains me with his love.

Unfathomable grace and mercy that's never-ending showers down
    on me,

I can never give him anything I have; I am nothing without my king.

Living a life of chaos, politics, and twisted scriptures pastors use,

The Bible says to tithe if you want blessings, and if you don't you lose.

A way of verses getting manipulated by truth from the savior,

How do you think that makes him feel? Are you the new dictator?

Trembling with thoughts I feel I can't overcome by the evil one,

Resist him, I say, *rebuke his attacks and watch him slither and run.*

Under my foot you go as I stomp you in the dirt and gravel,

I will look to my one true love and claim healing over my mind along
    with revival.

Amen, I say, thank you Lord for this relationship I hold so dear to
    my mind and heart,

Never again will I fear the things in this world, Lord, I give you my
    life, I will do my part.

Serving those around me with a love like Jesus, the ultimate perfect
    example,

The blessed oil that was covering you is an aroma I desire and crave
    for myself.

Just a taste of your aroma, I want to sense it and smell it in the air,

Let me rub oil on your feet like your servant Mary and wipe it off
    with my hair.

Teach me to love them the way you do, a love so powerful and strong
    it's to die for;

You died even for those you knew wouldn't enter that eternal life
    of salvation's door.
Never will we understand your ways over our own wretched thoughts,
Be my teacher, give me lessons and parables that I was never taught.
Subdue me in your presence through the dark of night when I am
    weary and alone,
How can it be possible you are always there, never having to leave
    your throne?
Thank you, Lord, for your son and holy spirit here on Earth in this
    coming time,
The day is coming, I can feel it, I am just waiting for the final signs.

My Groom

Never can I express what you mean to me in our lives right now;
You have always been by my side no matter the weather and drought.
You always found a way to cease and assist by the words of our Lord,
My book of pages hasn't been pretty, but you loved all of me, even
    the pages that were torn.
Always loving me with an underlying passion given by our King,
I can't fathom all the blessings he has given us, starting with the ring.
I remember what you said, about not having all the money in the
    world but giving me love to die for,
That's all I ever wanted; I just didn't think someone would wait
    for me outside my door.
Craving a love in this world is like trying to find a pin in a haystack,
Never thought a man would be able to bring the old goofy me back.
Making me laugh so hard that I throw my head back and snort, my
    face flushed,
Four months of dating, then you proposed—everyone thought it
    was a bit of a rush.
Knowing he gave us each other, how can we deny that,
He put you in front of me to lead me down his path.
I will always look back and remember the old times when we first met,
A girl so broken and nervous around you all I could do was fret.
One look you gave me and butterflies went crazy all around me,
Didn't think there was anyone out there who could truly
    appreciate and see the real me.
Yeah, I have baggage and things I need to work on and overcome,
That's where you come in and tell me my life of sin is done.
You always give me the best advice to help guide me in this world,
Look up verses, you tell me, and hear the pages in the Bible twirl.

My love for you is forever and I will always press harder in this
     walk with you,
One thing I can promise you is I will ride with you this walk until
     it's through.
My faithful servants, he will say at the golden gates when we come
     face to face,
Welcome to joy, peace, and love, he will say, *this was worth the wait.*
A faithful journey we had these seven years with trials and tribulations,
Now it's our time to meet our creator and thank him for his son.

STORIES

Home Away from Home

I have moved so many times that I have a memorized script to read to new neighbors. Due to my dad being in the Army, and constantly living near his base, it's hard to sustain long-term friendship. It was always hard to maintain friends at all my schools—I guess it was because I was always the new girl who started late every semester. I would attempt to talk to the popular crowd, which has always been my dream; to fit in and not be a loner sitting by the soda machine and dumpster.

Turning seventeen and moving to Beaverton, Oregon, I prayed for a good and fun senior year. Senior year is supposed to be the final and best year of our lives, right? I am originally from Los Angeles, in the state of sunshine, beaches, and short shorts on hot, sunny days. I am not feeling positive looking outside the window at this yucky, foggy, rainy weather. Do you want to know something worse? The school and town we moved to is called "Doomey Valley." Tell me why I feel like Kristen Stewart moving to Washington at the beginning of *Twilight*. Cliché, right? No, this is my life.

"We're almost here!" my mom said joyfully. Ugh, why was she always happy moving to new places? I think she's going through what older people call a "midlife crisis."

Pulling up, I saw a girl standing outside our house. "Who's that?" I asked my mom.

"Who's who, honey?" she replied.

"Hmm, never mind." I must have been tired from the thirty-six-hour drive. *Hmm, why did this house look familiar? I've seen it some-where before*, I thought. But after moving thirty-four times, all these houses began looking the same.

My mom and dad walked toward the door with some boxes while I scoped out my new environment.

"Hi, what's your name?"

Shaken by surprise, I turned around. "Oh, you startled me, hi. I'm Hope," I said.

"Oh my gosh, my name is Hope, too!" she exclaimed.

Ironic, I thought. She looked like someone I knew; I just couldn't pinpoint who. She was nerdy and goofy-looking, with crooked bottom teeth, but sort of pretty with her green eyes hidden behind her cheetah print black framed glasses.

"Since we both have the name Hope, you can call me Robin—it's my middle name," she said coyly.

"Um, sure, okay," I replied.

"There's one more thing I should mention," said Robin. "You know your house is haunted, right?"

What?! That explains why the agent sold it to us for 200,000 dollars cheaper than what it was posted for on Zillow.

"Well, I have to go unpack my stuff and get ready for my first day of school tomorrow."

"Okay," Robin replied. "We can walk to school together tomorrow!"

Oh, great, I thought, *my reputation is going to be ruined before it begins.*

***

BEEP, BEEP, BEEP.

My alarm clock didn't miss a beat before going off at 6 a.m. I struggled to get out of bed; I hadn't slept well, though I was not sure why. I opened my freshly steamed curtains from the night before and jumped back when I opened them. Robin was standing outside on my curb, just staring at me. *What's with this girl?* I thought. It felt like I was in the Twilight Zone.

I finished getting ready and kissed my mom goodbye. My dad was already at work, having left at 4 a.m.

Robin and I talked the whole way to school, about a fifteen-minute walk. I have never wanted to jump out in the middle of the road like I wanted to that very moment. Robin wouldn't shut up; all she would talk about was always wanting siblings and how not having her parents around was hard for her. She went on to tell me she wished she had a family like mine that she could come home to every day.

I walked into the school's main office, got my schedule, and found my first class. The high school was very small, with about 300 kids, so there were only five homeroom classes. I walked in, and for some odd reason, everyone was just staring at me like I had a monkey on my head or something.

Before I sat down, I noticed this adorable boy. During roll call, I found out his name was Fernando—wow, he was so cute. His beautiful, light brown, almond-shaped eyes looked at me while I went to sit down. It felt like there were a hundred butterflies in my tummy that were all trying to escape at the same time. I turned around because I felt someone staring at the back of my head. *Please let it be Fernando looking at me*, I prayed. I flipped my hair and turned around, and he did the unthinkable... He winked at me! *Oh my gosh, this is not happening*, I thought. Even though I had never done this before, I winked back, then quickly turned around. I waited a few minutes before looking back, and I couldn't believe my eyes.

He had a tic, meaning he constantly blinked rapidly with one eye and couldn't control it! Wow, just my luck.

As if it couldn't get worse, guess who was rubbing the back of his head, grazing her pointer finger all up and down his earlobe? Yup, it was Robin. I couldn't believe it; as soon as the bell rang, I quickly stormed off to my next class. I continued to the rest of my classes and couldn't wait for lunch. Of course, no one wanted to automatically be my friend or come talk to me, so I found Robin and asked her to sit with me. The smile on her face showed me a million things that she was feeling with just one smile. Kids were walking by, staring at me still.

"Why is everyone looking at us?" I asked Robin.

"Not sure," she replied. "Don't pay attention to them," she said.

Robin kept asking me questions, like what it was like to have a family and be an only child.

"It is okay, I guess, just wish I had someone to talk to when I am home alone."

"Good thing you found me," she replied.

"Yeah, I guess." Having Robin was better than nothing, even

though she did come off a little weird.

After school, I walked home by myself after I secretly waited around to see if I saw Fernando. *There he is*, I thought, *it's now or never*—but Robin had her arm intertwined with his.

How could he talk to her? She's weird, and not that pretty! At least I had blonde, curly hair, green eyes, and a decent curvy frame, something to look at. I guess I wasn't meant to have a boyfriend senior year. Maybe it was a good thing, and I would be like the girls who party every weekend, get high, make out with their boyfriends, and get pregnant right out of high school. I have to admit it would be nice to have someone hold my hand, kiss my cheek unexpectedly, and tell me I am beautiful when I am wearing sweatpants with his oversized T-shirt and my hair in a crazy tangled bun. Well, I can dream, I guess.

As soon as I walked in the door, I kicked off my shoes, put my feet up on my favorite cheetah-print pillow, and started playing Roblox. I was almost done with my race in Obi World when the doorbell rang.

"Who is it?" I shouted.

"It's me, Robin!"

I didn't rush to open the door, but as soon as I got up, she let herself right in like it was her home.

"Well, come on in," I said. Frustrated, I slammed the door behind me. "What's up?" I said.

"We need to talk," said Robin.

"Okay."

"You haven't wondered at all today why everyone was staring at you? Why I look so familiar? Why this house looks so familiar?"

"No," I said, but I did notice the hairs on my arms began to rise like an army ready for battle.

She moved closer to me, shaking, and I asked her what was going on. She stared deep into my eyes, and for some reason, I saw everything from the very beginning. It was like I was taken into a time warp or time machine, like *Back to the Future*, except for the old, cooky guy with Albert Einstein hair.

I saw my mom crying in her room. I walked in as soon as she left, and there it was, a picture of an ultrasound. What was odd was that it was an ultrasound with twins. *When did my mom have twins? I thought.*

"Keep searching, and don't open your eyes," said Robin.

Trembling with such fear and anxiety, I did what she asked as she squeezed my hands tighter.

I was in a womb and saw a baby next to me fighting for its life, a cord around its neck. I started feeling like something was choking me, too. I opened my eyes, gasping for air, clutching my stomach as I tried not to vomit.

"It's you," I said, "it's you! Wait a minute, this is the house where it all happened; why would my parents bring me back here? You're the reason we moved so many times—it had nothing to do with Dad's job. This house isn't haunted, but your mind is! You're my twin! If you died, how can I see you? Is that why everyone was staring at me? I saw you, but they couldn't. That's why they were looking at me. What's going on? I don't understand."

"You never will," she said. "Let me ask you something, Hope. Do you ever look down at your arms when you get dressed every morning?"

"No, why would I?" I looked down and saw abrasions all over my arms. "I don't get it," I said, "why would I do this to myself?"

"It's all in your mind, Hope."

I saw on my left arm four white bracelets that looked like hospital bracelets. Before I could ask Robin another question, I looked up, and she was gone. What was even weirder is that I was in a hospital room with my parents, who were crying, looking down at a bed, as a doctor said, "We tried everything from medication to restraining her to the bed."

"What happened?" my parents asked.

Confused, I walked over, and, to my terror, I saw ME laying in that bed with a cut artery in my arm, blood everywhere.

"We couldn't save her; by the time the alarm went off, we were too late. She cut four inches deep in her vein. I am so sorry for your loss."

"MOM! DAD! It's me, I'm right here!" I didn't understand what was happening.

"We reviewed the camera footage and saw that your daughter Hope was crying for someone to return and not leave her. You never noticed that your daughter was talking to herself, or suffering from depression?"

"No," said my dad, "we thought she was being a teenager, talking on the phone, hiding out like the other kids do."

My mom was clutching her chest with such pain and agony while tears rolled down her face, my dad squeezing her hand. The look on his face showed how badly he wished he could take my mom's pain away. My dad was always good at comforting and holding us while we were upset.

"There is one more thing," said the doctor. "She kept repeating a name over and over. Does the name Robin mean anything to you?"

My mom and dad looked at each other with their mouths open and the horror of a cold chill going up their spine.

"Hello?" I answered quickly.

"Hey, Fernando, it's Edgar, just calling to see if you have any work tomorrow?"

"Hmm, let me get home and check my schedule."

"Alright then," he answered. "Bye." *Click.*

I thought having my own business with workers would be a lot easier, yet that doesn't stop the endless thought cycle of God, work, family, ministry. I am grateful for what God provided, which is why I choose not to complain about a curse I have embraced with righteousness and integrity.

Ring, ring.

"Hey, Mammas," I answered. "What are you doing, beautiful?"

A quick, unseen moment passed in which I felt a huge smile from my wife on the other end of the line. "Nothing, just trying to clean up before you get home—how long before you'll be here so I can start cooking?"

"About fifteen minutes. I have to run into Home Depot real quick."

"Okay, babe, love you," she said, short but sweet.

She is everything that I needed to be complete after my relationship with my father. She has come such a long way; when we first started dating, she was still pretty fresh with anger and her wild mindset of paranoia and accusations. Now I wake up and see her trying and moving forward. Don't get me wrong, she has her moments where she explodes like a TNT bomb next to a match and gasoline.

I don't run anymore—I face things with her because I want to. We have four beautiful daughters, and my wife is going to university full-time online while taking care of them and managing a pretty decent household. I am very grateful to have someone like her in this rat race with me.

There's just one thing that bothers me about her. She always degrades herself and puts herself down. Yes, ladies, I can see after having several babies your body isn't the same, but do you have to complain about it? I wish she could see herself the way I see her.

Ring, ring.

Ugh, my phone never stops. I start pulling up to the house and see my daughters looking out the window. Though I can't hear their words, I know they're screaming joyfully, "Yay, Daddy's home!"

I open the door and they all run toward me like a herd of zebras running from a lion.

I look up and see my wife hurrying to put my mat and cup of ice at my seat. You know what's funny? Women go through so much to get their husbands' attention, whether it's a new perfume, body spray, hairstyle, whatever. That's when women want to be noticed and called beautiful and sexy. To be honest, when she has her hair tied up, wearing my old T-shirt, running back and forth to wash the dishes, and yelling for the girls to clean their room is when I admire her the most.

She is the most beautiful when I see her determination to serve her husband and her kids; that is a mission in itself and I think she's amazing for that. Yet she seeks a fleshy desire from me, like when she gets a new pair of pants or underwear she wants to show me. Yes, I desire her in that moment, not in a moment of lust but a moment of intimacy between myself and the most beautiful woman I have set my eyes on. She doesn't see what her life and blessings have turned into due to her obedience and faithfulness to our Father. She is more than a cute face and body; she is a daughter of the most high, a princess of the King, and my queen.

Interrupting my thoughts, she asked if I wanted more tortillas.

"Yes, babe, I eat everything with tortillas," I replied.

She giggled. "Well duh, you're Mexican," she replied.

"No, baby, I am a Chi-canooo," I said pleasantly.

She rolled her eyes. I came behind her and just held her for a second. Though smelling of breast milk and sweat, it still didn't stop me from embracing my best friend and partner.

As the house settled, I sat with my family and turned on our weekly *Star Wars* show.

"Again!" cried Nevaeh. "Why do we have to watch this again? We see this all the time!"

"Go to your room, then," I replied, "you have a TV in there." I laughed because she just stared at me with a cold stare.

Hours later, and I guess I passed out because I looked up and saw my wife in her sleeping shorts and a tank top that barely covered anything. We went to the living room, and she just grabbed my hand and started kissing me. Before I had a chance to ask her what was going on, she just told me to shut up. Well, can't argue with that—we ended up having the best time together just enjoying what comes along with marriage, intimacy and adventure.

Before going to bed, I leaned over and thanked her.

"Thank you for what?" she said.

"Thank you for being you, and moving forward with your life fighting for us."

She turned around and kissed me. I felt the tears well up in her eyes through my chest. "You're all I ever wanted," she said.

I couldn't help but hold back tears. I have never been so happy in life thanks to the Father.

I kissed our girls good night, ready for whatever came my way the following morning. "Thank you, Father," I said before I shut my eyes.

***

The next morning, I woke up to my alarm going off late. I huffed my way out of bed and into the shower. "Dang it," I shouted.

My wife, next to the baby, woke up. "What happened, babe?" she asked.

"My alarm didn't go off. I need you to remember to turn it on—that's your job," I yelled. I looked over at her. She looked pissed yet hurt at the same time. "Can you get my cooler ready?" I asked her.

Even though I could tell she didn't want to, she got up, put her glasses on, and walked out of the room. In that moment, I hoped she would walk right into the wall. I know I shouldn't think like that, but I was just upset.

She packed my cooler and went back to bed. As I started my beat-down old truck, I couldn't help but think of how easy it is to get mad at the same person who will still be there for you and do the same daily routines as they did when they weren't mad at you.

I called her and told her that I was sorry and I didn't mean to get upset.

"I was just trying to help you," she said. "I am sorry too."

Whew, what victory we found in that moment together as a couple and team. I hung up and couldn't help but be grateful for her. Yeah, she has her moments, yells and gets frustrated, but at the same time she is the only person here on Earth after my father that I could count on for the most part.

I have to remember I am not the only one who gets upset easily and struggles through my daily life. I had a talk with my wife and realized how much she holds inside just to put a happy face on for me and our girls sometimes. I have to remember to appreciate all the little things in life and live every day accordingly. To think of how she has the little strength she's got to wake up and still push through her day while I am going through my daily tasks. I have to remember we are a team and neither of us is alone on this journey.

She is definitely ashes turned into a diamond.

The Woman in the Window

"Oh wow, this place is beautiful, darling," said my girlfriend.

"Yes, love, it is. Will be nicer if you were to stay with me."

She opened her eyes with surprise. "Christopher, are you saying you want me to stay here with you? Like, move in?"

"Of course, love, this is why I asked you."

"I can believe this—well, I actually can, darling, because at the possibility of you asking I packed half of my things, which are sitting at the foot of my stairs in the apartment."

"There's one more thing," I said as I turned around and got on one knee.

"What are you doing?" she exclaimed.

"I want to spend the rest of my life with you. Will you take this forever walk with me?"

"Yes, yes!" she exclaimed.

We both had been waiting for this night, wearing out our purity. It was on from there.

I can't believe how surprised Natalia was; we have been together since grad school and we supported each other through all of it. She changed her major every few months until she realized she wanted to be a veterinarian and save animals and care for them. I didn't mind—I made enough to support both of us while she got to do what she loves. She loves animals and I love making money and splurging it on my queen.

Shaking my head with laughter, I just hugged her and put my nose to her neck. She wore this amazing cotton candy-scented perfume that I couldn't get enough of. As she moved toward me to kiss me, I pushed her back and pointed to the room. She nodded and walked sensually to the room as I followed like a puppy following its owner. It wasn't dark yet but I didn't think anyone could see inside. This was the day we both had been waiting for almost six years.

I had yet to hang up curtains and arrange my bed, but can you blame me? I work 24/7 and am CEO of a multibillion-dollar company selling Tupperware. Yes, Tupperware. Believe it or not, women go ape-shit over that crap.

I pushed her toward the bathroom and started to take my shirt off, then yanked her silky shorts off and turned her around so she was facing the mirror and it just took off from there. I loved every moment; she had the softest skin that made me want to just rub her all over with oil and massage every part of her body.

After we finished, we got dressed and saw someone looking through a window across the building.

"Christopher, who the hell is that? There's just some lady staring at us."

We ran out of the room and finished getting dressed, a bit shaken up at having been caught in the act. I wondered how long that weirdo was standing there.

"It doesn't matter, darling, let's call the moving company to get your stuff here first thing in the morning."

"Alright, love, I will go home and finish packing."

"Call me when you're there," I told her.

"You shouldn't worry about me," she responded, "you're the one I worry about." She hugged me and planted a delicate kiss on the cheek that gave me butterflies.

As she walked out to her car, I waved and blew her a kiss. As I turned around, there was that woman from the window, but she wasn't an ordinary woman—she had a face that didn't look real, a little waxy but beautiful. I tried to walk up to her, but as I got closer she dissipated into the air, leaving a foul odor behind of old leaves soaked in mud that had been drizzled with day-old piss.

I must have been tired if I really thought she disappeared into thin air, but Natalia had seen her too. I decided to just grab a burger from our spot and get some zucchini. I had worked up a bit of an appetite during playtime. As I was ordering, I saw the woman from the window again.

What the hell, man, am I tripping? Is this one of those crackheads that can do tricks with their pipe smoke? I wondered. I turned around, ignoring it, and ordered my food, went home, ate, watched the end of *Fast and Furious*, and passed out.

I woke up to my phone ringing.

"Hello?"

"Why didn't you call me last night, Christopher?!"

"I am sorry, darling, I grabbed some food and passed out."

"Well, you can just make it up to me later, then," she said flirtatiously.

"Anything for you, darling."

"Well, my movers will be there in an hour, so I will finish getting ready and head on over."

"Alright, then," I said and hung up. I took a quick hot shower to wake up, and when I came out of the shower there was that woman again. *Oh my gosh! I can't take this anymore.*

I got dressed and walked to the building from which she was spying. As I approached the building, I started to get chills all over. It was an abandoned building.

"Wait a minute," I said to myself, "how is this possible?"

There were bars on all the doors and windows. I didn't understand what was happening. I had to go back to the apartment and call Natalia.

When I got there, it was locked. *Great.* I couldn't find the keys in my pocket—what the hell was going on? As I turned around, I saw Natalia approaching.

"Thank God, darling, I locked myself out. Do you have the spare key?"

She blatantly ignored me.

"Darling! Can you hear me? Did I do something wrong? Hello?!"

"Love?" she said. "Is that you?" She turned around and kissed another man in front of me.

"What the hell—are you kidding me? Wait a minute, what's going on?!"

She walked into the room with him and I couldn't believe what was happening. There were wedding pictures of Natalia and this guy together plastered all over the walls like a damn photography studio.

But wait a minute—the woman from the window was in a picture with someone I knew...it was me! This didn't make sense; I literally was just with Natalia.

"Why do you still have this guy's picture, Natalia?" said the unknown man.

"I guess I forgot it was in there, sorry, love."

I walked closer to the picture with the woman beside me, and it clicked. She was my nurse back in grad school. I had gotten in a horrible accident and she helped me with my therapy. The last memory I have of her is being inside the...wait, I remember the hospital near my treatment center caught fire with me and her in it. They couldn't figure out how it happened or why. I remember feeling this tingling, numbing sensation all over my body.

I looked over and saw a newspaper that read *"Unknown fire at treatment center in Philadelphia."*

I heard laughing; it was Natalia speaking. "I can't believe we never got caught, my love."

"How could we? I am a known paid arsonist, just known at an underground level. Now we have all the money we could ask for, ha ha ha."

Wait—if I died, how am I seeing this right now?!

My nurse Michelle looked at me and said, "It's the portal to the other realm. Since we are dead, we are living with the dead—we must go back. I was just able to grant you one ticket to go back in time and you chose the day you proposed to Natalia. You don't remember at all what happened at the burger shop?"

"No," I replied shakily.

"You were ordering your usual zucchini when I ran into you there. I was gonna order pastrami, but that's when the fire started."

"What fire?"

"Not sure how it happened," she said. "Out of nowhere there was this huge *kaboom*. Before anyone could react, the fire blew through the windows and that was it."

"What realm are you talking about?" I asked.

"Well, growing up you hear about dying and coming back as spirit or just a floating body no one can see. There was a secret realm in that burger shop. That's why when we died we entered the portal to a place where we can still live our lives, just with others who died in that fire as well. It's freaky, I know," she said, "but we didn't ask for this, we just so happened to be ordering food at the wrong place at the wrong time. Took me years to realize where I was and why. The owner told me he was top of his class, a scientist at Harvard in '94. He created a time warp for people who passed over so they can still visit the living. Just in a way where we can't be seen. That's enough talking, though, our pass is granted for only twenty-four hours and you have one hour left. Let's go."

She pointed to the building across the street where I always saw her. As we walked back, I was still tripping out on the fact that I was dead and imagined everything I had just seen.

"Let's go," said Michelle, "we have more people to visit from our past. Let's go see your mother."

"Wait, my mom died when I was born."

"Exactly," she said. "She's in the unborn realm; she's waiting for you."

"Umm, okay," I said unsteadily. "What do I have to lose if I am already dead?"

Bullied Girl in the Corner

"I can't believe you don't believe me, Mom."

"You expect me to believe that these girls beat you up because of your hair color?"

"Mom! Why would I lie? I get beat up at home, so why should school be any different, huh?"

"You always play the victim," my mother replied.

"Well, I must be one if I play the part right, huh?"

Gosh, I swear my mother acted so stupid sometimes. I knew she wasn't dumb, so why play the part of idiot?

Anyways, let me introduce myself. I am Sadie, I am ten years old, and I am a bully's number one target. Not just a bully at school but at home as well. My stepdad doesn't like me too much—I don't know why. I did everything he asked me; I made him sandwiches and did good in school, yet there was always a punishment ready to be handled.

I never knew what being hit was like because my mom never beat me. But I guess when you get remarried, all the responsibilities go to the husband because mothers are too weak for anything. Like my mom in this case.

I wasn't ready for school the next day. There was a group of four girls that was in attack mode every day to basically stone me with their words. You know that saying "Sticks and stones will break my bones but words will never hurt me"? That's a crock of shit because words hurt me way more than a belt across my behind. That was a line my teacher liked to use, but my teacher wasn't the one being called vulgar names due to my skin color and looking different from everyone else.

I literally couldn't wait to go home on days I knew my grandma was going to take care of me. She was the best grandma and we did everything together; she was my best friend and the one person who I could talk to and trust. I was walking home when I saw her waiting by my front door, waving, saying, "Sadie! How was school?!" I don't know what she was screaming for—I was like ten feet away from her.

I ran up to her and hugged her. She asked how school was again and I shrugged, acting like I couldn't hear her. She looked at me as if she could feel my pain and all the horrible thoughts in my head. She grabbed me and just gave me one of those good hugs where you can let yourself go and cry your heart out, not caring how you sounded or if you snorted while crying.

"Let's get McDonald's," she said.

"Really?" I asked. "Yay!" I was excited because they were giving out Furbies with the kids' Happy Meals and I only needed two more for my collection. Plus it was nice to escape the torment of my ten-year-old life. I swear sometimes I felt like I was fifteen with all the crap I was already going through.

We got to McDonald's and had the best time ever, until the ride home, when I tensed up and my grandma seemed to notice.

"What's wrong, my love?" she asked.

"I don't want to go home," I said. She knew all about my step-dad and felt my hurt.

"If you need me, call me—I will be right upstairs."

We lived in New York in one of those crappy houses with stairs outside to get to the second floor—weird, I know. They must have been high when they created that house.

As we pulled up, I saw my stepdad parking the car. I couldn't help but be scared.

My grandma kissed me and I walked out of the car with my Furby. I walked into the house and he was sitting there, watching soccer with a beer and bolillo in his hand.

"Who said you can go with your grandma, huh?" he scolded.

"Mom said I can go because you and her were working late."

"Did you drink one of my sodas?" he asked.

Oh great, I thought, *I drank like three.* "No," I said.

"Don't lie to me," he said.

"I'm not lying," I said, lying.

He stood up and walked away.

Hm, that's weird, I thought. Usually he would have hit me by now. *Oh no—I spoke too soon.* I heard the belt snap from across the room. My cheeks were already tingling from the burning and numbness I was about to feel.

"Did you drink my soda?" he asked again.

"No," I said, scared.

He pulled my pants down and hit me with the belt as I screamed in instant pain.

"Don't lie to me," he said.

I had to stick with my truth of a lie. It was too late to go back now.

He made me pull my pants back up and said, "We're leaving."

"Where are we going?" I asked.

He said he was going to take me to the police station so the cops could give me a lie detector test to see if I drank his soda. He said I was going to be in big, big trouble.

As we were walking to the car, I yelled, "I drank your soda, I'm sorry!"

"Go to the house," he said.

I ran to my bunk bed, relieved and scared at the same time. He told me to get off my bed and slapped me across the face so hard his handprint stayed there for about an hour.

"I hate you," I yelled. "You're not even my dad—my real dad isn't here and you're not him."

He slapped me again. At that point, I didn't care anymore. I took off running out the door, not knowing where I was going. Little did I know my aunt was standing outside; she heard me yelling and ran after me. She grabbed me and told me she loved me and it was okay.

"Why doesn't anyone love me?" I asked her. "My mom lets him hurt me, she doesn't love me, and my stepdad doesn't care about me because he likes to hurt me and make me cry. It's like he enjoys seeing me in pain, crying and screaming for help."

My aunt had gone through some similar things, so she was

good at comforting me. It still didn't make me feel any better—maybe it should have, but it didn't. Being so young, I didn't understand why I deserved all of that bullying and abuse. I literally was just a ten-year-old girl trying to find outlets and ways of keeping myself happy, so I wasn't miserable all the time.

Bullying isn't okay. People who never got bullied don't understand the outcome of being hurt internally by other kids their age. Youth should be a happy time making friends and messing up artwork, not being mean to other people because it makes you feel better.

Maybe someone out there will read this and understand my message. I will say one thing to all my bullies: What doesn't kill me makes me stronger. I am covered, and that's all that matters.

PERSONAL ESSAYS

Beauty from Ashes: My Story, Your Glory

Are you looking for a raw testimony? A story that has traumas, dysfunction, terror, and distortion? Well, you found it—I am going to be completely honest and uncut writing this story. This is for my heavenly Father's glory in my life; he deserves everything because he saved me from this black fifty-foot hole of shame, fear, rejection, and feeling unloved. There is a twist to the story, so make sure you read to the end if you want to know how great and big our God is.

I don't know if I would say I had a decent childhood. It was just me, my mom, brother, grandma, and aunt for a while, living in this two-story apartment in Boyle Heights, Los Angeles. My dad wasn't around while I was growing up; he was going through a dark time, struggling with drugs and family issues. Little did he know that while he wasn't around, I was going through the same struggles—family issues, anyway.

I don't remember exactly how my mom met my stepdad. All I know is everything moved pretty quickly between them, from what I remember. One day he was sitting on our couch, and the next he moved in. At first I thought, *Wow, I am finally going to have a dad.* I thought I would be like the other kids at school waiting for their dads to pick them up.

Little did I know I was going to experience some things I never imagined.

My mom never hit me or laid hands on me. That wasn't her nature at the time—she was a good mom, working hard to support and take care of us. I can't remember what I did or if I even did anything, but he came into our lives when I was about six years old. I remember him getting mad at me for something. He made me pull my underwear and pants down and he slapped me on my butt. I didn't understand what was happening, wondering, *This is new to me—what's going on?* I was crying for my mom because she was supposed to protect me. Boy was I wrong.

Let's be honest: we aren't all perfect. I am not justifying her actions, but she went through her own battle of generational curses. So eventually this became a normal part of my and my brother's life. If we talked back to my mom or stepdad, if we were smart alecks, didn't pick up after ourselves, etc., we received punishment. Eventually it got worse—he started slapping us in our faces, still pulling our pants and underwear down, hitting us with sandals, belts, his hands.

I will admit I had a smart mouth, and as I got older I couldn't take it anymore. He wasn't my dad; why was he doing this? The worst part about it was my mom didn't seem surprised or like she cared at all. This happened from when I was six to fifteen years old. Can you imagine going through that kind of trauma?

He and my mom had two kids after me and my brother. He never once laid hands on them. Never! Another thing that might seem odd is that I don't have a memory of him sexually abusing me, but I grew up acting like a victim of someone who was abused. Later down the line, I had a couple of people confirm that the way I acted was possibly due to suppressed memory of sexual abuse. He always made me feel uncomfortable, but the crazy thing is I would have to act like I loved him sometimes just to get a treat or something I wanted.

A punishment for me doing something wrong would be wearing ugly clothes to school, and shoes that were way too big, because he knew I would get embarrassed. Everything he did was so that I would get embarrassed and ridiculed. This went on for so long that I felt like taking my own life. Once, I was walking by our van outside, and one of the rearview mirrors was broken, so I got a piece of glass and started cutting my arms everywhere. Something about cutting myself at the time physically relieved me. That wasn't enough to get my mom's attention. They sent me to a counselor, I told them about the abuse, and guess what? No one did anything about it.

I can't imagine seeing my kids go through something and not try to help them. I grew up thinking it was my fault. Let me tell you guys who are going through abuse or who have overcome it: It is not your fault. It was never your fault. This is where the enemy likes to fill our minds as a young child going through abuse and being vulnerable.

Let me tell you the truth. God is always with you; he will never forsake you. It is written! God turns every dark thing into the holiest of lights. God did a number on my life and he deserves all the glory. If you feel unloved, rejected, alone, depressed, anxious, hungry, be hungry for the word of God. Read the book about God's love for you and how much you mean to him. You won't find the answers to your questions in any other book but the Bible, and the letters of confirmation and humility.

We will never understand the love our heavenly Father has for us. It is similar to a parent's love for their child, but there is a difference—we are all God's children because he created us and put us in the wombs of our mothers that he chose for us.

John 3:16: <u>For God so loved the world that he gave his only son, that whoever believes in him should not perish but have eternal life.</u>

This verse tells us that God gave up his only son Jesus Christ for all of us sinners in this world. Now think about this for a second. Jesus is the son of God, and God gave him up for all of us to have eternal life, have a relationship with him, and walk the path as a follower of Christ. Would you sacrifice your only child for the world to have a second chance? It's a tough truth to swallow, but that is how much God loves you! He gave up his son, saw him suffer, crying out for him, saying, "My God why have you forsaken me?". He watched him swallow his own blood and hang on a cross, which had the sins of every person in this world weighing on him. We should have been on that cross and dealt with the punishment. But no, God wanted to show us his greater love, which is beyond our understanding. His grace, his mercy—that's a lot to take in, huh? Want to know the best part about his gift of everlasting life? It is free! You don't need an admission ticket or to be holy, because none of us are perfect except Jesus the son of God. We are given a chance at restoration, forever joy, peace, and happiness to be with our savior. It all starts with giving him our heart.

Even as a child, I knew there was a God, but back then I didn't know what I know now. He never left me; he gave me strength as a child to endure my trials, to be the child of God I was destined to be.

God was working on me before I was born. I allowed him in my life at a young age because I didn't have anyone to be there for me. Little did I know he was holding my hand while my other one was wiping my tears.

God turned my dark childhood into triumph and gave me strength, and now this trauma he turned into triumph to help heal others in the mighty name of Jesus Christ of Nazareth.

AMEN!

God, Are You Real?

I have gone through so much. Every time I broke, even super glue could not save me. Growing up, so many people were around, but no one was there to listen to or see me. How could I go through this, and no one understood me, not even my mother? You hear that parents are supposed to protect you, but mine did not. She did the total opposite; she hated me growing up. Scars visible and hidden—which would matter more to you? The hidden ones hurt the most because we are the only ones who know.

My first stepdad screwed me up, from name-calling to occasional slaps to the face to aggressive bare-bottom hitting with belts, leaving a welt that hurt to sit on. I am not lying. I told my mom she never listened to me; I do not know if she ignored my cry or did not care. Going through physical abuse is just as bad as mental and emotional abuse. Physical abuse is temporary, but mental and emotional sticks with you until you are older. I still struggle with self-esteem issues because of all the crap that I went through. Whenever I see a little kid crying, I wonder what happened to her. Does she have a mean stepdad who abuses her when no one is around?

I went from abusive stepdad to an abusive boyfriend to putting myself in a compromising situation with a man who used and abused me. That is when the drugs came in. I hit a point where I felt worthless, ugly, stupid, useless, an extra body just looking for love that no one gave me. I took many pills one day and laid on a bed with my eyes rolling back, ready for death. I did not care if I lived; I was at a point where I did not have anyone who cared about me or loved me.

Boy was I wrong; I searched my whole life for a love that would die for me, one so powerful I could not contain the joy I had in my heart.

I saw the room spinning, ready to close my eyes one last time, prepared for death. Something inside me yearned to fight this feeling I was having. I thought there must be something more for me than drugs, a life without love, a life wandering alone. The next day, it all changed. I got arrested, and my mom picked me up from jail. I had not seen her in a couple of years; she had put out a missing person's report, which surprised me because I did not think she cared. I lost my glasses getting beat up by these men at a bar the night before, and even without glasses, I still saw her from afar. She brought some lady with her from some women victims' group.

They asked if I had drugs in my system and asked what had happened. Even though my mom honestly did not care, I still held her like she had not been the horrible mom she was to me. I still love her to this day; she is my mother. God gave her to me for a reason, and I forgive her. It took me a long time to understand what forgiveness meant. I had such a hate toward her that when she would call me, I instantly got anxious, my body heating up, and I would feel sick to my stomach. God saved my life, and he used my mom. God made that known to me. He used the person I felt anger and hatred toward to soften my heart.

I went to a program to get clean and start a new life. I did not realize how much I used alcohol and drugs to mask my feelings and hide the pain I felt all these years. Let me tell you, feeling real emotions is hard. I would wake up sad for no reason, and one slight smell would trigger me into my childhood or a situation that I had just gotten out of. It was hard; in those moments, I would take a shot or some pills, and the euphoric feeling would surpass everything that I felt in that moment. I still struggle to this day. God must help me 24/7. Without him, I do not know how I would survive.

God gave me everything I wanted in life growing up, but I was not perfect when God saved my life, and I never will be. I have always wanted kids and someone to love me. I was just scared because I let my guard down before, and I got hurt every time. It is funny because I told God I wanted a man to love me; I did not care about money or material things. *Just give me someone who will love me forever.* That is what he did; he gave me the desires of my heart; he gave me a man who calls me his queen and has given me a love to die for. God did so much for me that I could not help searching for more of him and what it meant to know God and do his will.

I have learned I will be forgiven because God loves me, and I will never be perfect, but that is okay. I help young moms in my situation; who better to help those girls than me, a victim who is now a victor? The story's moral is to forgive those who hurt you the most, so you do not carry that burden for the rest of your life. God knows what you need and the desires of your heart. If he changed me, there's hope for you.

Adventure of a Lifetime

I remember sitting down, wondering why I went through what I did to get where I am now. I've always struggled with my past, shame, and guilt for poor decisions being made. I turned twenty-six on a hot summer day in Phoenix, Arizona. I would never get through this heat, I thought. I had already gone through fiery trials, so I knew I would be okay. In a compromising situation, I could never live with myself knowing what I did. Then again, he saved me. *He?* you might ask—wait until the end to find out.

I never thought I would be in a program to save my life; I just wanted love. Is that so wrong to ask? A love that would die for me, a love that was so strong you hear about it only in fairy tales. I remember seeing him walking by on the property of the program. Wow, was he cute. I had seen cute guys in my life, but something about him made me turn around and say "HI!" I can't believe I did that. Want to know the worst part? He looked away from me like I was chopped liver! *Wow,* I thought. I had never been rejected like that.

His name was Fernando. He had light brown skin, beautiful brown eyes that glossed while the afternoon sun shone on them, and a medium build. He wore an old-fashioned hat like men wore on the runway in Paris. He was so handsome.

I should've known better that no one would ever love me. Time went on, and my relationship with this person grew; I would stop talking to him as soon as someone stepped into the room. This person I speak of is the realest thing I have ever felt. He was the person who I would go and go to; sometimes, I would ignore him and disregard his wishes, but I didn't care then. I wanted to do my own thing.

The love I wanted was before me; how could I deny that? His passion was so strong that even when I made mistakes, he would still call me and hope for a call back. Either way, he never left my side.

I had the best relationship I have ever had, but I knew there were more things I needed to do to grow in this friendship. I needed to change my ways; I had a potty mouth, and I would judge people and look at them with disgust, focusing on negative things.

The program I was in offered me a job at a thrift store, which I took because I told my secret person I would do it for him and do it for free. People thought I was crazy working five days a week for eight hours a day and for nothing in return. They didn't understand my desire to make him happy.

Fernando came in one day, which blew my mind; I had him out of sight and out of mind for a while because I was focusing on another relationship. When I saw him in that huge truck, I ran, put on some cotton candy spray, fixed my frizzy, straight hair, and put on lip gloss. I ran back outside with the manager and said, "Oh, what's he doing here?" I knew this was a crazy sign.

He seemed to be just as surprised as I was. He wasted no time asking to hang out with me. I was embarrassed to tell him I was still in the program. I was sneaky and got my way a lot. I looked through my manager's phone, took his number from her contacts, and called him that night. He was shocked, but something moved me to do it. I liked him and was drawn to something about him.

Time went on, and we got to know each other. I came to find out he knew my secret person, too; I thought I was the only one who talked to him among the fake people and noise around me. Finding someone else, looking for this love you hear about in fairy tales, was thrilling.

The unthinkable happened: Fernando asked me if I wanted to marry him, and without a doubt, I said yes.

"You should know one thing," he told me. "I am on this journey, and I take it very seriously. Are you willing to walk this path with me?"

"What are you talking about, weirdo?" I joked.

He still had a severe look on his face. He said, "God comes first in my life, and if you can't accept it, I can't be with you."

"I want to follow God," I said.

Fernando told me I would have to leave everything behind me and look toward the finish line of my race. I was so confused, but something in me wanted what he was talking about; he grabbed my hand and said "Are you ready?"

I took Fernando's hand and never looked back. I have never been happier; God is so good to me when I don't deserve it, and let me tell you—this has been a crazy, thrilling adventure. Knowing he will never leave or forsake you, always having someone in your corner, is promising and will be the best adventure of your life.

God promises us a future of hope and not to harm us. He has never failed me, and he won't forget you either.

This adventure is to be continued and forever ongoing. I hope you will also say yes to it. Will you take his hand as he holds it before you?

About Atmosphere Press

Founded in 2015, Atmosphere Press was built on the principles of Honesty, Transparency, Professionalism, Kindness, and Making Your Book Awesome. As an ethical and author-friendly hybrid press, we stay true to that founding mission today.

If you're a reader, enter our giveaway for a free book here:

SCAN TO ENTER
BOOK GIVEAWAY

If you're a writer, submit your manuscript for consideration here:

SCAN TO SUBMIT
MANUSCRIPT

And always feel free to visit Atmosphere Press and our authors online at atmospherepress.com. See you there soon!

About the Author

LILLIE DIAZ is originally from Los Angeles, California, and now lives in Phoenix, Arizona. She is married to the most wonderful man, Fernando, with whom she has four beautiful daughters. She grew up with a rough childhood and her outlet has always been writing. She earned her associate's degree in creative writing from Paradise Valley Community College in May of 2024 and is currently working on her bachelor's degree in English at ASU. She hopes to write all kinds of books to glorify God—she wants to tell others about his wonders and what he can do in their life.

www.ingramcontent.com/pod-product-compliance
Lightning Source LLC
Chambersburg PA
CBHW020722150726
48196CB00028B/786/J